The Lion Book of *Five-Minute* Christmas Stories

Told by John Goodwin

Illustrated by Richard Johnson

LION
CHILDREN'S

Contents

The Lion Book of Five-Minute Christmas Stories

For Linda J.G
For Grandma, love R.J

A Lion Children's Book
an imprint of
Lion Hudson plc
Wilkinson House, Jordan Hill Road,
Oxford OX2 8DR, England
www.lionhudson.com
UK hardback ISBN 978 0 7459 4943 7
UK paperback ISBN 978 0 7459 6926 8
USA hardback ISBN 978 0 8254 7807 9
USA paperback ISBN 978 0 8254 7941 0

First hardback edition 2007
First paperback edition 2009
This printing July 2009
Hardback: 3 5 7 9 10 8 6 4 2
Paperback: 1 3 5 7 9 10 8 6 4 2 0

A catalogue record for this book is available
from the British Library

Typeset in 18/24 Lapidary 333 BT
Printed and bound in China by Printplus Ltd

Distributed by:
UK: Marston Book Services Ltd, PO Box 269, Abingdon, Oxon OX14 4YN
USA: Trafalgar Square Publishing, 814 N Franklin Street, Chicago, IL 60610
USA Christian Market: Kregel Publications, PO Box 2607, Grand Rapids, MI 49501

Mary and the Angel

In the little town of Nazareth, a young woman called Mary is sewing her wedding dress while sitting with her mother.

MY MOTHER is lovely but sometimes she does go on a bit.

'It's so exciting, Mary,' she said. 'There will be ringing bells, laughing, dancing and such feasting.'

'Yes, Mum, I know,' I said, trying to think about sewing my wedding dress.

'You're going to be so happy. Your wedding day with Joseph will be the very best day of your life.'

'Yes, Mum.'

Then she pulled a parcel out of her bag.

'Just a little present,' she said.

'But it's a whole week yet to the wedding,' I replied.

Inside the parcel was a bundle of baby clothes.

'What have you bought these for?' I asked.

'Oh Mary, you used to look so sweet in clothes like those.'

'No, Mum. I don't want them.'

'I'm so looking forward to being a grandma and having a tiny little baby to cuddle.'

'Stop it, Mum, you're doing my head in. I'm not even married yet.'

I had to leave the house and get a bit of fresh air. That's when it happened. I saw a bright golden glow in the sky. In the blink of an eye, the light grew into the shape of a face. I was trembling, it was so scary.

'Don't be scared, Mary,' said a gentle voice.

As I looked up, there was an angel smiling at me. Yes, that's right. An angel.

'Hello Mary,' said the angel.

'How do you know my name?' I asked, my body still trembling.

'I'm God's messenger, Angel Gabriel.'

I opened my mouth to speak but no words came out, so I pinched myself to make sure that this was really happening.

'God is pleased with you,' said Gabriel.

'Is he?' I said.

'He has sent me to tell you some amazing news. Mary, you are going to have a baby who will be very special indeed. You will have a son.'

'A son?' I repeated like a parrot.

Gabriel smiled. 'Call him Jesus,' he said.

By this time, my head was swimming. 'How can I have a baby when I'm not married?' I said. 'Surely that can never be.'

'God has chosen you, Mary,' said Gabriel. 'You're going to give birth to God's very own Son. His Holy Spirit will visit you. Everything will turn out well. You'll see.'

'How will everything turn out well?' I asked.

Gabriel looked at me and smiled again.

'How?' I asked.

Gabriel's smile turned into a huge sunbeam that filled the sky with a golden glow. Before I had a chance to ask him anything else, the sunbeam faded and he was gone.

Everything was back to normal – or so it seemed. The sky above my head was still as blue, and through the window I could see Mum still gazing at the baby clothes. Mum! How was I going to tell her? I went back inside and picked up her present. Immediately, she began to grin like a big cat.

'Oh Mary,' she said. 'It will be brilliant being a grandma, and

you'll make such a lovely mother.'

I took a pair of tiny baby mittens out of the parcel and repeated Gabriel's words to her.

'Everything will turn out well. You'll see,' I said. And I just knew it would. ❧

Joseph's Dream

Joseph is a carpenter and was planning to be Mary's husband. When she tells him about Gabriel's visit, he's really worried and cancels the wedding.

USUALLY WHEN I'm doing jobs in the workshop with my apprentice, young Clem, he doesn't say much, but today I couldn't stop him talking.

'I've heard you're not going to marry Mary then, Joseph,' he said. 'What a pity. I was looking forward to your wedding and having a party.'

I carried on sawing some wood and stayed silent.

'They say Mary was visited by an angel,' he went on. 'Is that true, master?'

Still I said nothing.

'Sounds strange to me,' said Clem, staring hard at me. 'I've never heard of an angel coming to Nazareth before.'

My hand slipped on the saw, and Clem could see it was shaking.

I sent him home early, making an excuse that I didn't feel well, and carried on trying to work until it was late. How could I explain to Clem what had happened? He'd never believe me. The wood kept slipping in my hand, and every time I picked up the saw I missed the wood and cut my hand. The hammer felt as heavy as a block of stone and soon became impossible to lift. My eyes were as heavy as the hammer, and all I wanted to do was to close them and go to sleep.

Maybe I did close my eyes, just for a second perhaps, because the hammer began to move and the saw was cutting the wood by itself without my hand doing anything. The work was being done by no ordinary human but an angel workman with golden wings, and the room was aglow with light.

'Come on, man,' said the angel in a quiet voice. 'You've got to believe Mary. She's telling the truth, you know. God has chosen her to be the mother of his Son. Everyone will call him Jesus. That means 'God saves us', and when he grows up that's exactly what he'll do. You know Mary loves you, Joseph. So stop being daft and marry her. Look after baby Jesus as if he were your own son.'

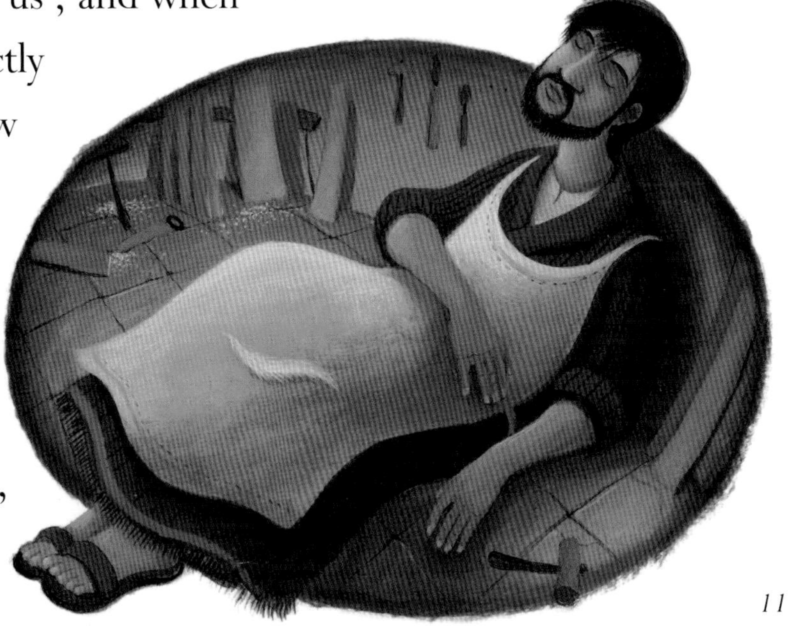

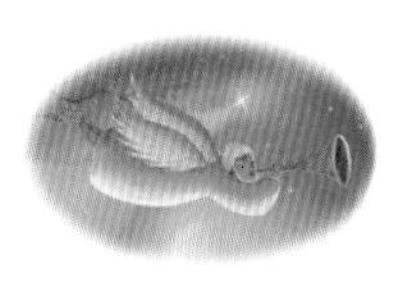

I jolted awake but the angel had disappeared. Everything was still and calm. All my carpentry tools were back exactly where they belonged.

'So much for dreams,' I thought, looking for the piece of wood I'd been working on. Not a stick of wood was in sight, but instead there was something much more grand. Resting on my workbench was a carved wooden donkey on tiny wheels, which was quite the most perfect creation you ever saw.

I went straight to Mary's house with the carving under my arm and knocked excitedly on her front door.

'Go away. It's very late,' called a sleepy voice from inside the house.

'Mary… it's Joseph… just look out of the window,' I shouted.

'Come back in the morning. I'm tired.'

'Please, Mary. It won't take long. I've got an amazing surprise for you. Just come to the window.'

The moon came out from behind the clouds just as Mary's face appeared at her window.

'Look at this,' I shouted, holding up the carving. 'It's a gift from God. Our baby's first present.'

Mary stared down in silence.

'Did you make that?' she finally cried.

'No,' I said. 'Not me but…'

How could I tell her it was all God's work? Was now the moment to say just how much I loved her and of course I'd marry

her? Should I describe the toy wooden farm that I'm planning to make for the baby, complete with carved sheep, an ox and a goat?

But before I'd found the right words to say any of this, Mary had rushed downstairs and put her arms tightly round me. It was the very best hug I'd ever had. ❧

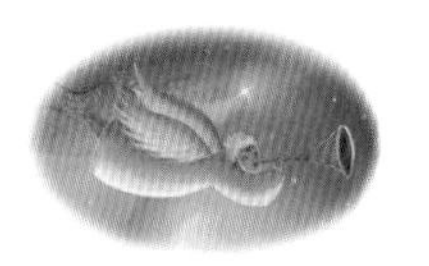

The Journey to Bethlehem

It is bitterly cold winter weather. Mary and Joseph have to travel to Bethlehem and Mary is expecting to give birth to baby Jesus at any time, so their journey is a tough one. She rides on the back of a donkey, who gives us this story of their travels.

HEE-HAW. Who'd be a donkey? The miserable cold winter weather makes my whole body ache. Hee-haw. I wish I were human. My master and mistress, Joseph and Mary, are complaining that they have to go all the way to Bethlehem just because the Roman emperor wants everyone to sign a register for his new tax. It's me that will carry the luggage and Mary too. I wish someone would carry me there. Can you imagine that? A human carrying a donkey? It'll never happen, will it? The journey was three days' work, eighty thousand steps.

The first day was bearable, and we covered miles and miles. Joseph walked ahead, leading the way, and I followed with Mary riding on my back. That night we had a good supper and slept out

under the stars.

The second day was when the troubles began. We soon came into the hilly country with steep climbs. It wasn't long before Joseph began to take rests and moan.

'My feet ache,' he said. 'How much further is it to the top of this hill?'

'You only have two feet, Joseph, and I've got four of them, so that's twice the ache,' I hee-hawed. He didn't listen to me, of course. Humans never do.

'I've got a stiff back too and my bag is so heavy,' he grumbled, and then he promptly dumped his bag on my back.

Now it was the final day. I hee-hawed onwards up steeper hills. I held my head up high as snow began to fall. Silence out on the long road. No birdsong today, just the sound of straining breath. Mary was so tired she could hardly hold onto my back. Steady now. Easy does it. One slow step at a time.

It was late in the day and now the sun was setting. Joseph stumbled badly and fell, twisting his knee so that he couldn't even walk. I bent my head down to look at him and I could see it was serious. I licked his face as

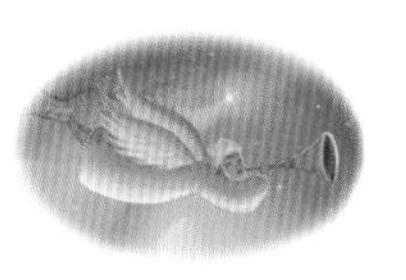

he lay on the frozen ground where he'd fallen, but he didn't move.

Suddenly everything had changed. I could see that it was up to me now and me alone. If I didn't do something fast, disaster was going to strike. I licked Joseph a second time and he lifted his head, but he was still on the ground. I swung my tail close to his hand and he gripped onto it. I tried not to grimace as he pulled himself onto his feet, still holding my tail.

'We'll move on,' he mumbled.

Mary was at the very end of her strength.

I bent my knees and nuzzled Joseph gently. Somehow he slithered onto my back too and I was carrying all three.

A new calm came over me. Mary and Joseph had put their trust in me.

They'd chosen me above all other animals and I would not let them down.

Though my back may have ached from the heavy load and my feet were sore from the stony ground, I'd never show it. Not now. It wasn't the time or place. The only thought that was important was to lead them – baby, Mary and Joseph – safely into Bethlehem.

I hee-hawed up to the top of the hill. I made every step forward as gentle as possible. No stumbling, lurching or bumping. Slowly onwards. I would not fail them. Hee-haw, three steps more. Four, five, still alive. Six, seven… and we'd reached the top of the hill. Below us now the lights of Bethlehem shone out on the other side of the hill. Let your heart never fail.

We had succeeded. Praise be to heaven. Baby Jesus will be born in comfort now and not out on the open road. Mary gave me a gentle pat, and turning my head I nuzzled her hand. ❧

No Room at the Inn

When Mary and Joseph arrive in Bethlehem, their problems are far from over. Finding a place to stay the night in the crowded town is almost impossible. An innkeeper's wife describes what happens next.

ALL WEEK our inn had been heaving, not with local people but folk who had travelled from far and wide. If I'd had fifty pairs of hands instead of one, I'd still not have had enough to serve them with all the food and drink they asked for.

'A jug of wine good woman, if you please.'

'Coming sir,' I shouted.

'Can we have your best date tart, landlady?'

'Right away madam,' I cried.

'We need a bedroom for the night, with a view of the town.'

'Sorry – there are no beds to be had at any price,' I called. 'Not for love nor money.'

I was carrying two jugs of wine in one hand, a flagon of mulled pomegranate punch was tucked under my arm, and in the other hand was a plate of very flat fish.

There was the sound of a loud camel spitting out in the yard. Camels are such disgusting creatures, and so dirty. It's their spitting that gets me down. Their owners park them in the inn yard and walk off, leaving their camels without a thought for all the trouble they cause.

The next thing I knew, the spitting camel had broken free and was loose in the inn. My husband's hand reached out to grab it but he missed and caught me instead. Up went the fish in the air, down went both jugs to smash on the floor, and down fell the flagon, spilling the punch like there was no tomorrow.

From out of nowhere, a traveller holding on to a donkey caught

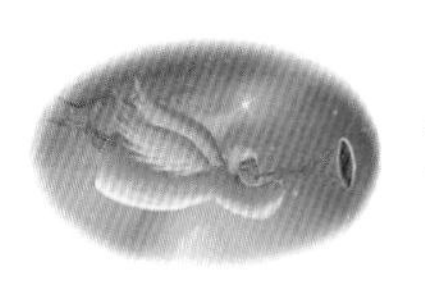

the end of the camel's rein and brought it under control.

'Nice one,' I said, taking hold of the rein.

Just then I noticed standing beside him a young girl dressed in blue, who looked like his wife. She had the sweetest smile you ever did see and was so serene, with the most beautiful face. I could see she was heavily pregnant and trembling with exhaustion. Her husband put his arm round her, trying to support her as best he could.

I found myself ignoring the broken crockery and moving towards her.

'You'll be needing a bed for the night,' I said quietly.

'There are no beds here, as well you know,' snorted my husband.

I pretended I hadn't heard him and led the two travellers gently out at the back of the inn, where the air was cooler. We went across to the stables, and by now the poor girl could hardly walk.

'It's not brilliant,' I said, pulling open the stable door, 'but it's the best I can do for you.'

As soon as they were inside, Sooty, our black cat, began to purr proudly and I knew they'd be safe for the night. Caribell, the ass, brayed and Thomas, the dog, wagged his tail as a sign of welcome to the weary travellers.

'So kind,' said the girl, still smiling.

'There's only straw for bedding,' I said, 'But it'll keep you warm.'

I left them there and walked back into the inn to pick up the broken pieces.

Later, when it quietened down, I took a blanket off our bed and went back to the stable with it. The girl's husband had brought their donkey in too and all the animals were wide awake, standing guard around them. The girl had her eyes half closed and she was smiling as peacefully as you like at her newborn baby. ❧

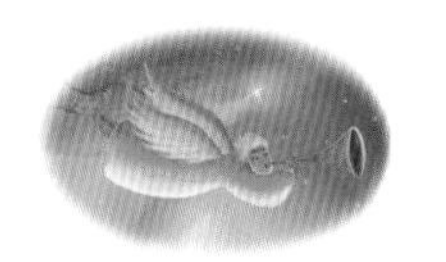

The Angels

The angels are meeting in heaven for choir practice when Gabriel asks them to decide how to break the news of the birth of baby Jesus to all mankind. Grace, a quiet angel, describes what is happening.

WE WERE IN the middle of choir practice when Angel Gabriel gathered us all together.

'The birth of baby Jesus is to be one of the most important days there has ever been,' he said. 'It is our job as angels to give a sign for this very special occasion. We have to let mankind know the great news.'

'We could use white feathers,' said Angel Thomas. 'A single white feather is a sure sign of the visitation of angels.'

Gabriel smiled as only an angel can.

'A lovely idea,' he said. 'But I fear they would be too flimsy. Earthly storms blow feathers away in an instant,' said Gabriel. 'This is the birth of our great saviour. We need something magnificent.'

'Let's fly down to earth,' said Angel Angelus, before opening his mouth even wider to sing his very top note. 'The earth people would be truly amazed to see us. They would stare in wonder.'

'But everyone would be terrified to see and hear so many of us,' said Gabriel. 'There'd be chaos on earth, utter panic.'

'Oh, do let us go. It will be great fun,' said Angel Alfa.

Gabriel flapped his wings just a little.

'Do any of you have any other ideas?' asked Gabriel. 'I was hoping for something very special indeed.'

There was silence in the heavens and nothing stirred. No angel's wing fluttered or flapped. After a few heavenly seconds, which are much longer than seconds on earth, Gabriel spoke again.

'There is little time left for us to decide,' he said. 'Jesus will be born this very night, and already it is growing dark. Look down now and see…'

With a wave of his arm, Gabriel parted the great curtain that separates heaven and earth, and all of us angels peered down to earth. We could see blue sky and below that the dark outline of houses with a few lights already lit in windows. The shape of a simple wooden shack stood out and inside it Mary and Joseph were already asleep, worn out by their long and tough journey. Gathered around them were a group of animals, keeping guard quietly.

Before we could see any more, Gabriel let the curtain close and it blocked out the earthly scene in the stable.

'Time is almost up
and it seems we have failed,'
said Gabriel. 'I shall have to see
God immediately and speak to him. I'll
tell God that, in all the company of angels
not one of us has succeeded in making a
perfect plan. Not a single angel has thought of a
suitable sign to announce the birth of our saviour.'

As Gabriel sighed and rose from his seat, a voice was heard. I knew it was now or never, and trying to make my voice as bold as I could, I said, 'I have an idea.'

All the angels looked round at me and Gabriel beamed a huge smile.

'Speak, Grace,' he said. 'Maybe the shyest and quietest angel in our company has the best plan.'

'Our angel choir is something very special,' I said. 'When the trumpets sound out, and the harps and lyres and cymbals add their own magic, it is heavenly indeed. Add to that the music of all our angels' voices in full unison, and you have the perfect way to celebrate the birth of Jesus.'

Gabriel's eyes gleamed.

'Perfect,' he said. 'Our choir of angels shall sing at the very place where Jesus is born, and the music will sound out over all the earth.'

'Can we join in with all the carol singing on earth?' asked Angel Angelus. 'We could wear scarves and woolly hats as a disguise so the earth people wouldn't know we were angels.'

'Maybe,' replied Gabriel. 'I'll have to think about it.' ❧

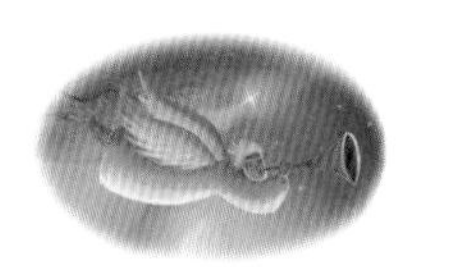

The Young Shepherd

On the night of the birth of baby Jesus, shepherds are out on the hillside with their sheep. This story is told by a young boy who is spending his first night alone with his flock.

OUT ON THE open hillside at midnight, it's pretty scary. That's when I like to call out the names I've made up for our sheep. It's a good way for us shepherds to keep ourselves awake.

'Eye Bright, Snub Nose, Waggle Tail, Woolly Back.'

But already my eyes felt heavy, and all I wanted to do was to fall fast asleep. So I pinched myself hard and shouted out some more names.

'Thick Snout, Wriggle Foot, Muddle Patch.'

Today was a big day for me. It was the first time the other shepherds had left me alone to look after the sheep. While they were tucked up warm and cosy in their beds, I was by myself under the big black sky.

'You can do it, boy,' said my father as he smiled at me. 'Just take it easy. You're ready now for your first night alone.'

Sheep are steady most times, but when the mood takes them they can charge about like crazy. It just takes one and the rest will follow, running about until they hurt themselves trying to jump over walls, or getting their heads stuck in trees and bushes. That's when I imagine their bleats are sheep words and I talk back to them. It calms them down and it helps me too.

'Baaa,' say the sheep.

'Yes it is cold,' I say.

'Bleat bleat,' say the sheep.

'You've got bellyache? Me too,' I reply.

'Bleat bleat baaaa bleat,' say the sheep.

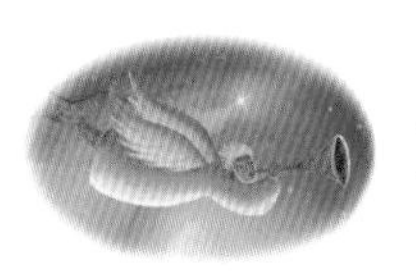

'I know it's pretty boring eating nothing but grass, but what do you expect me to do about it?' I shout.

The light in the sky had already started to fade. Soon it was so dark that you couldn't see your hand in front of your face. I kept telling myself that I needn't be afraid to be alone out here when it was pitch black. You can always smell sheep, see their eyes shining, sense their bodies, hear them breathe, and they know you're there for them.

I sat down by a thorn bush and I must have dozed off to sleep for a few moments. Suddenly, I woke with a start and opened my

eyes to see the sky was full of golden light. Then a voice said, 'Don't be afraid, good shepherd.'

My heart was thumping as the voice continued, 'It's time to rejoice. This very night, a king is born in Bethlehem who will light up all darkness. He is called Jesus. Go and find the animals who are keeping guard over him. Baby Jesus is lying in a manger.'

As I looked up, the golden light changed into angels' wings, which spread across the whole sky. The world was full of the most magical and beautiful music you ever heard.

'Glory to God on earth,' sang the angels. 'Peace is come to all people.'

As suddenly as they had appeared, the angels vanished, the music stopped and once again I was alone on the hillside. A small nose pushed itself into my hand and a tongue was licking at my fingers. I knew it belonged to one of the young lambs. Then a strange bleating started amongst all the sheep like I'd never heard before. It was as if they were talking to each other, trying to explain the happenings of the night.

Down below, men's voices were shouting up towards me.

'You there, boy?'

'Hello, young lad? Did you see the angels?'

It was the rest of the shepherds coming to find me. We all set off immediately to see if what the angels had said was true.

And it was. ❧

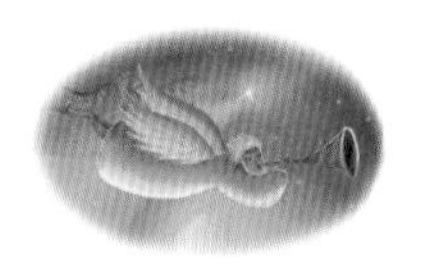

King Herod and the Three Wise Men

When Fezulk, a security guard in King Herod's army, sees three strangers arrive at the royal palace, he senses that a deep mystery is about to reveal itself.

AS SOON AS they walked towards the palace gates, I knew they were no ordinary visitors. All three of them were wearing the grandest clothes, made out of the finest silks and golden thread. King Herod had given me orders to check out any strangers, and if you want to keep your head you always obey him.

Immediately I went out to inspect the visitors.

Usually it's me that asks the questions, but before I could open my mouth one of them said, 'Where is the newborn baby king?'

'King Herod is our only king here in Jerusalem,' I said firmly.

'We have seen the baby king's star in the sky…'

'We have come to worship this new king…'

'Stop there,' I said. 'Give me your names please.'

'Balthasar, Caspar and Melchior,' they answered. 'We are wise men of the east who have travelled very many miles following the bright new star.'

I told them to wait by the gates and went to see King Herod. He wanted to see them immediately.

At first, he was in one of his smarmy moods, all greasy smiles and grins.

'Welcome, welcome to my palace,' he said, throwing his arms wide open.

Then the wise men began to repeat what they'd said to me, only this time in more detail.

'A new star must be a sign of something very important.'

'Surely it must be bringing us some wonderful news.'

'We believe the birth of the new star tells us a new great king has been born, and we have come here to honour him.'

Herod's face changed from greasy white to bright red and then to thunderous black. He began to thump his hands together, and when he does that it means big, big trouble. I bit my lip, held my breath and waited for the fireworks to start, hoping it wasn't me who was going to be burned alive.

Herod looked at the wise men again and, swallowing hard, tried to make his thumping fists stop thwacking into each other.

'There is no king here but me,' he said, 'and I'm hardly a baby, am I, Fezulk?'

'No Your Majesty, you're not a baby,' I muttered.

'You must be very tired and hungry after such a long journey,' he said, as the grovelling grin returned to his face. 'My servants will look after you.'

Before the wise men could protest, he clapped his hands and left the room, dragging me behind him.

'Fetch the high priests. I need them here immediately,' he hissed as soon as we were outside the room. 'Tell them to bring every chart and scroll they possess.'

As soon as the priests were all gathered he said, 'There have been stories that a great new king will be born one day. Where is this so-called "saviour" to be born?'

'In our scrolls it is written that the place will be Bethlehem, Your Majesty,' they replied, bowing so low they nearly scraped the ground.

In a second, they were dismissed and the three wise men brought back in.

'Go to Bethlehem and look for the baby king,' said Herod quietly to them. 'And when you've found him, please come back here and tell me, so that I may worship him too.'

As soon as the wise men had gone and I was left alone with Herod, he went utterly crazy. He pulled my sword from my belt and waved it frantically in the air, shouting, 'Come back soon, wise men, so that I can… kill… that baby. There is only one king here and there always will be and his name is HEROD!'

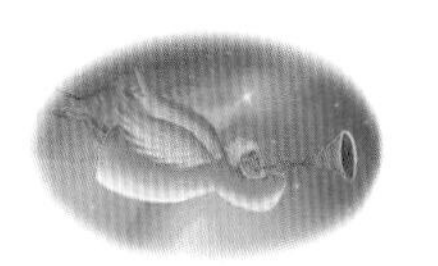

The Warning Dream

Balthasar, Caspar and Melchior leave Herod's court and follow the bright star in the sky to Bethlehem, where they find baby Jesus. Their rejoicing is cut short, however, by a strange dream. This story is told by Balthasar.

OVER HILLS we climbed. Along lanes and tracks we wandered. Round mountains we travelled. Through deep woods we stumbled.

'I thought our journey was finished yesterday,' said Caspar as we came out of the wood.

'I'm exhausted,' muttered Melchior. 'How much further is it to Bethlehem, Balthasar?'

I looked up into the sky, which was just growing dark, to see that the wondrous bright star had already appeared.

'Not far now that we have the star to follow,' I answered. 'It is a kindly eye looking down on us that's been our guardian ever since we left home.'

Though we were all exhausted, on we travelled and at last reached the town called Bethlehem.

'I feel sure this is the place,' I said. 'Let's ask.'

We called at the first tent we saw.

'Good day, friends,' I said. 'We come in search of a newborn king.'

The family in the tent closed down the tent flap abruptly and wouldn't speak to us. It was the same at the next place we tried, and the next.

'I feel faint for lack of food,' said Melchior. 'Let's go into that inn at the end of the street.'

The inn was very busy.

'We have travelled many miles,' I said. 'The brightest star in the sky shines directly overhead. Has a special baby been born here?'

The innkeeper's wife looked at the three of us and smiled gently.

'Come with me,' she said, and she took me by the hand and led us to a wooden shack at the back of the inn.

As soon as we stepped inside the tiny stable, we all knew our journey had not been wasted. Lying in an animals' manger was the most perfect, smiling baby you have ever seen.

'A king of a baby,' whispered Caspar.

'This is the great event, to be sure,' said Melchior, sinking down to his knees.

'At last the promised one is here,' I said quietly. 'Our newborn king is come.'

There was silence in the stable and nobody moved. Then a cat purred and a dog wagged its tail.

'Presents… we have presents for the little one,' said Caspar to the baby's parents, who were close by the manger.

We'd brought special presents for the baby and laid them down before him. We gave him a tablet of gold, frankincense, which is a sweet smelling oil, and rich perfume called myrrh. Then, rejoicing, we left the family in peace.

That night a terrible dream woke me up.

'I saw King Herod in a horrible dream last night,' I said to the others.

'That's strange. So did I,' cried Caspar. 'A voice told me not to go near him again.'

'I heard that voice too. It warned of great danger to the baby and said we should go back home another way,' said Melchior.

We decided immediately to find a different track home that would take us many miles from Herod's palace. Before we began the journey, we returned once more to the baby king and his parents and warned them of the dangers we'd seen in our dream.

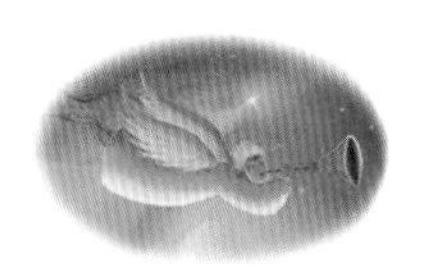

Saving the Baby

News of the birth of a baby who is the most important king ever travels fast. Fezulk, the security guard in King Herod's army, along with many others is given the job of hunting down all baby boys.

KING HEROD stamped around his palace, roaring at the top of his voice. 'I'm the mightiest king in the world! The greatest! How dare they say that a new king has been born? It is nonsense!'

Then he'd shout, 'Who am I?' and we had to repeat, 'The only one, Your Majesty. The greatest ever,' as we bowed down before him.

You wouldn't think it could get any worse but yesterday it did. Three wise men were supposed to visit him for a second time and tell him about their visit to Bethlehem, but they didn't show up.

'They're not here?'

'No, Your Majesty. It is reported that they've gone home another way.'

'Another way? Another way?' screamed Herod, trembling in

rage. 'Wise men indeed – wasters, more like. I don't need them anyway. I can sort out this little problem. In fact, all little problem baby boys called Joshua and Joseph and Cain and Zechariah and any other name under the sun. My soldiers will find them and finish them off.'

He sent for us all, and we had to swear an oath to carry out his order or lose our own lives. It was the little children or us. That's the way Herod is.

Most of us were sent to Bethlehem.

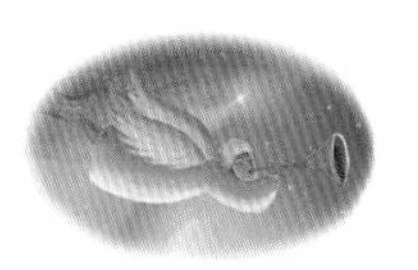

'Search every tent, every building and every street. Look into everything and then look again. Don't come back until you've found something.'

Herod offered a rich reward to any of us that could find this king baby.

I went off on my own and found the inn straight away. There was a strange quiet about the place. I was suspicious immediately.

I snooped around and came upon a little wooden shack you wouldn't have even known was there unless you were looking hard. It was dark inside, and at first I thought the place was deserted. Then a dog growled and I put my hand to my sword. By then, my eyes were getting used to the darkness and I could see two people with a baby, sitting in the midst of a circle of animals.

Stepping forward I said, 'I'm looking for...'

But I didn't ever finish that sentence. The baby's eyes found me. Trusting, clear eyes that looked into my heart. My sword fell out of my hand.

'You're in great danger,' I found myself saying. 'They plan to kill you. You must all leave Bethlehem immediately.'

We placed the baby in a basket with clothes covering his head so that he was hidden.

'Follow me,' I said to the baby's father and mother, lifting the basket into my arms. 'Stay silent and I'll help you to safety.'

At the end of the first street we met another of Herod's soldiers.

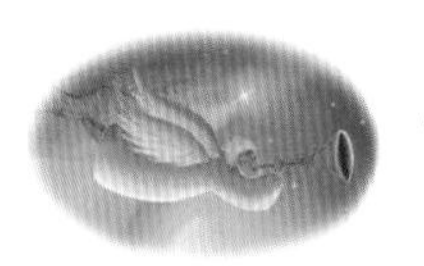

'Step aside there,' I said. 'We have important news for King Herod.'

The soldier looked at my security badge and let us through.

In the second street another soldier blocked our way with a sword.

'What's in that basket?' he shouted. 'Everyone has to be searched on this street. No exceptions,' he said.

'Food,' I replied. 'Let us through immediately.'

At that moment the baby began to wriggle about in the basket, and the soldier saw.

'Food doesn't wriggle,' he said, pushing the tip of his sword into the basket.

Suddenly there was trouble at the other end of the street. Someone was running wildly, shouting and crying out. The soldier turned and moved off towards the disturbance.

I turned, took hold of the basket and headed out of the street, not stopping until I had left the town. Then, in the quiet darkness, I handed back the basket to its rightful owners. I took one long last look at the tiny baby's face before I left the three of them. ❧

The First Christmas Tree

How will you decorate your Christmas tree this year? Will you use sparking lights? This is the story of the very first Christmas tree and is told by a fir tree deep in a wood.

IT WAS A bitterly cold day and the ground was as hard as iron. I was shivering from the depths of my roots to the tips of my cones.

There was a sound far off on the edge of the wood.

'Listen,' called the holly tree in a prickly voice.

The noise sounded again, only this time it was louder and closer.

'It's coming this way,' said the sycamore.

'Footsteps. It's footsteps,' cried the chestnut.

Then we saw them. Two small figures, huddled close together for warmth, were walking slowly through the wood.

'Look,' said the larch. 'One of them is carrying a baby.'

'A baby so small,' whispered the willow.

'Too cold. Too cold,' hooted an owl high on a beech tree branch.

The couple came to a halt in our small glade. We could see that one was a man with a beard, and the other must have been the baby's mother, with a blue shawl. The baby looked so tiny and its clear eyes were wide open. The couple looked first this way and then that way, but still they didn't move.

'They must be lost,' said the oak. 'They don't know which way to go.'

The mother reached out a hand to try to pull the blanket a little tighter round the baby's body.

'The baby will freeze to death,' worried the wild cherry.

Just then a fleck of snow drifted down on the wind, followed by another and another. The sky grew greyer by the second.

'They're shivering,' said the sycamore. 'And soon it will be dark.'

The spindle tree tossed its slender head and shook its slender trunk. Its scarlet berries jangled.

'We must do something. Do something,' it cried.

'What can we do?' whispered the willow, weeping a little.

'If only we had legs,' said the larch, 'we could run to make a shelter for them. But all our roots are fixed in the earth.'

'All my leaves have fallen,' sighed the oak. 'I can't offer them any protection against the bitter cold.'

I looked at the baby again with my evergreen eyes. It was now or never. I reached out with my branches and gave them a shake. A few of my cones fell to the ground. The mother's head turned towards me and so did the tiny baby's, with eyes wider than ever. Then they came to me and sheltered under my bushy branches. I let my branches lower slowly, slowly, round them and soon the baby was fast asleep.

'Well done, fir tree,' whispered the willow.

'Amazing,' announced the ash.

The sky grew darker and the snow came thicker, but they were safe now.

'Perfect bliss,' I said to myself, and a little tear fell from my eye. Soon the tears were flowing freely and there was nothing I could do to stop them. But as they fell they didn't spill onto the sleeping travellers. Oh no.

As the tears trickled downwards they froze in long icicles all the way to the ground.

Early next morning the sun came out and the icicles shone like bright jewels in the clear air. When the baby opened his eyes, my sparkling gems were the first thing he saw. The sparkle shone in his eyes too and, looking up at me, he smiled. ❧